Theory Paper   Grade 5   2018   A
Model Answers

1

(a) (i) (3)

Mozart, Piano Sonata in D, K. 284

etc.

(ii) simple (1)

duple (1)

(iii) (2)

etc.

(b) (i)   Chord **A**   IV   root / IVa (2)

Chord **B**   II   3rd / IIb (2)

Chord **C**   I   5th / Ic (2)

(ii) acciaccatura / grace note / crushed note (2)

2 (a)   augmented 2nd   diminished 12th / (6)
compound diminished 5th   perfect 4th

(b) (4)

3 (10)

4 (10)

(a) **adagio** means:

slow ✔

at a medium speed ☐

gradually getting slower ☐

held back ☐

quasi means:

always ☐

as if, resembling ✔

nothing ☐

so much ☐

calando means:

singing ☐

dying away ✔

hurrying ☐

calm ☐

attacca means:

prominent ☐

go straight on ✔

in strict time ☐

with movement, agitated ☐

subito means:

simple, plain ☐

always ☐

suddenly ✔

in the same way ☐

(b) (i) 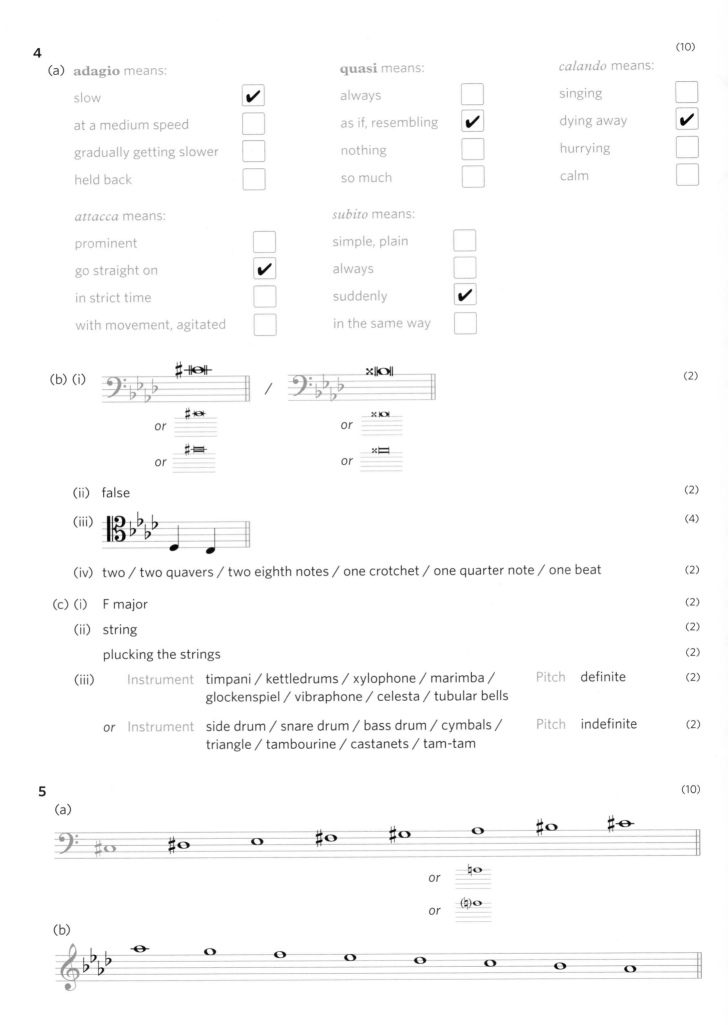 (2)

(ii) false (2)

(iii) (4)

(iv) two / two quavers / two eighth notes / one crotchet / one quarter note / one beat (2)

(c) (i) F major (2)

(ii) string (2)

plucking the strings (2)

(iii) Instrument timpani / kettledrums / xylophone / marimba / glockenspiel / vibraphone / celesta / tubular bells   Pitch definite (2)

or Instrument side drum / snare drum / bass drum / cymbals / triangle / tambourine / castanets / tam-tam   Pitch indefinite (2)

5 (10)

(a)

(b)

6

(a)  (2)

(b) X mediant (2)

    Y leading note (2)

(c) true (2)

(d) seven (2)

(e)  (5)

(10)

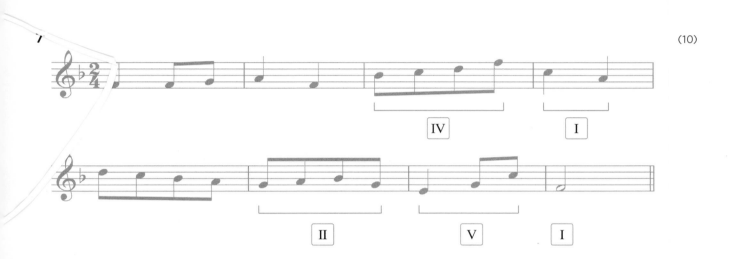

Theory Paper   Grade 5   2018   B
Model Answers

1

(a) (i)   (3)

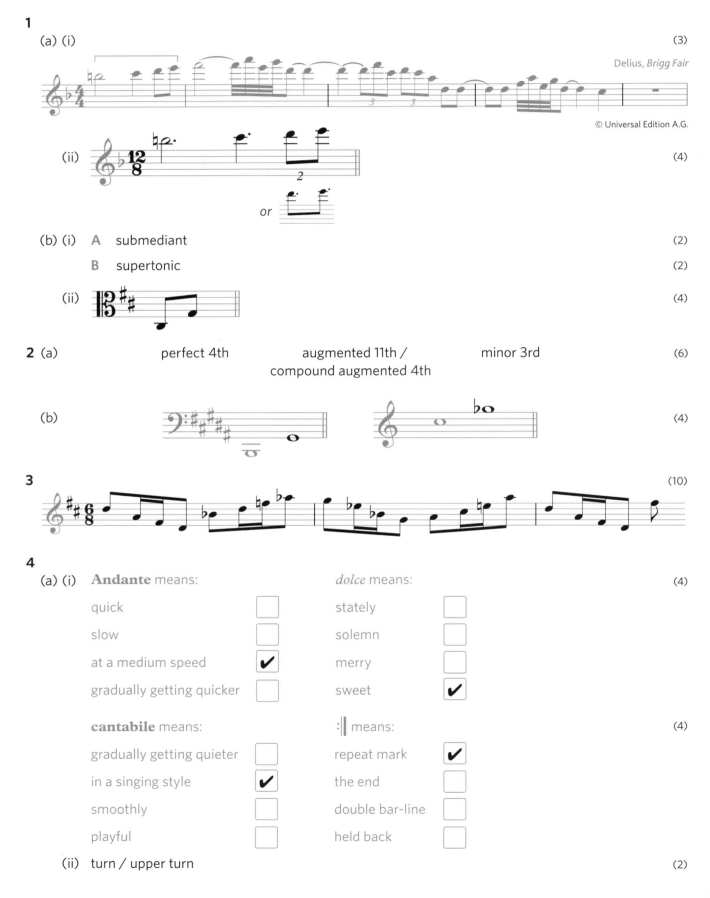

Delius, *Brigg Fair*

© Universal Edition A.G.

(ii)   (4)

or

(b) (i)   **A**   submediant   (2)

       B   supertonic   (2)

(ii)   (4)

2 (a)   perfect 4th   augmented 11th /   minor 3rd   (6)
                                  compound augmented 4th

(b)   (4)

3   (10)

4

(a) (i) **Andante** means: *dolce* means: (4)

quick	☐	stately	☐
slow	☐	solemn	☐
at a medium speed	✔	merry	☐
gradually getting quicker	☐	sweet	✔

cantabile means: :‖ means: (4)

gradually getting quieter	☐	repeat mark	✔
in a singing style	✔	the end	☐
smoothly	☐	double bar-line	☐
playful	☐	held back	☐

(ii) turn / upper turn   (2)

(b) (i)   Chord **X**   II   5th / IIc   (2)

   Chord **Y**   IV   3rd / IVb   (2)

(ii)   *All possible answers are shown on the extract reproduced below.*

   B   Bar 5   (2)

   C   Bar 4   (2)

   D   Bar 7   (2)

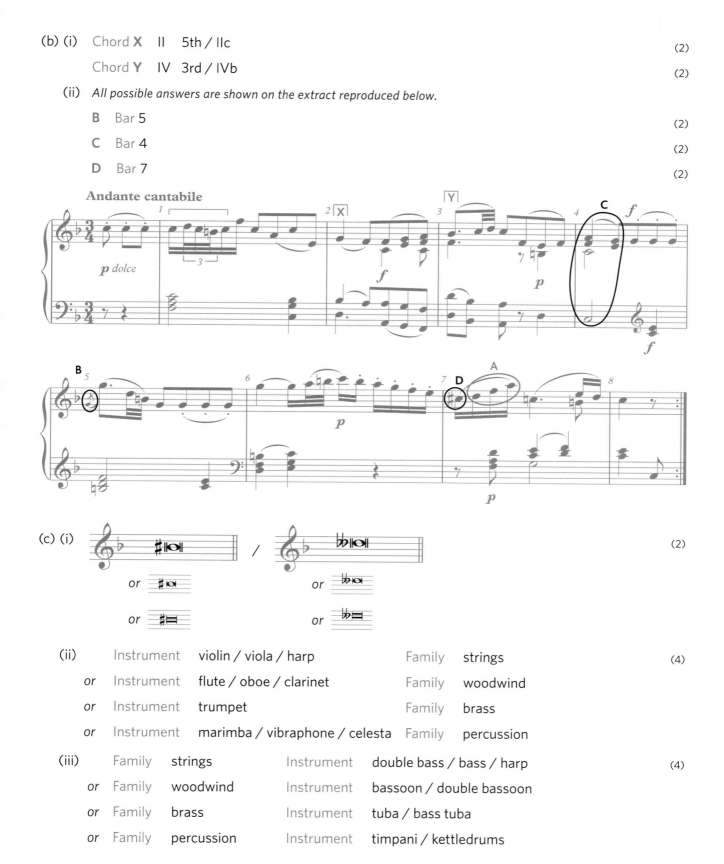

(c) (i)   (2)

(ii)   Instrument   violin / viola / harp   Family   strings   (4)

   or   Instrument   flute / oboe / clarinet   Family   woodwind

   or   Instrument   trumpet   Family   brass

   or   Instrument   marimba / vibraphone / celesta   Family   percussion

(iii)   Family   strings   Instrument   double bass / bass / harp   (4)

   or   Family   woodwind   Instrument   bassoon / double bassoon

   or   Family   brass   Instrument   tuba / bass tuba

   or   Family   percussion   Instrument   timpani / kettledrums

5   (10)

(a)

(b)

6 (a)    (2)

(b)    (3)

(c) E flat   (2)

(d) *All possible answers are shown on the extract reproduced below. For full marks candidates need to identify only one example of the answer.*   (2)

(e) true   (2)

   true   (2)

(f) twenty-eight   (2)

7   (10)

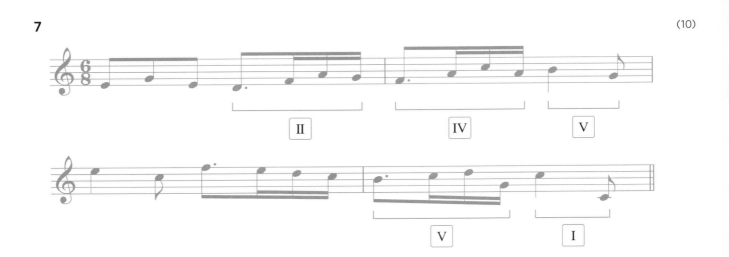

Theory Paper   Grade 5   2018   C
Model Answers

1

(a) (i)   (4)

Bloch, *Schelomo*

or **2/2** / **C** / **¢**

(ii)   Bar 3   (2)

(iii)   (3)

(b) Chord **A**   I   5th / Ic   (2)

Chord **B**   II   3rd / IIb   (2)

Chord **C**   V   3rd / Vb   (2)

2 (a)   minor 6th   major 7th   augmented 5th   (6)

(b)   (4)

3   (10)

4

(a) (i)   **Nicht zu schnell** means: *ad lib.* means: (4)

not too slow		at choice ✔
getting faster		in the same way
getting slower		agitated
not too fast ✔		becoming more lively

(ii)   (4)

(iii) B minor   (2)

(b) (i) twenty-eight (2)

(ii) false (2)

true (2)

(iii)  (4)

(c) (i) tenor (2)

(ii) Instrument violin / viola / cello / harp Family strings (4)

or Instrument flute / oboe / cor anglais / clarinet / Family woodwind
bass clarinet / bassoon

or Instrument trumpet /horn Family brass

or Instrument vibraphone / celesta /marimba Family percussion

(iii) Definite pitch timpani / kettledrums / xylophone / marimba / (2)
glockenspiel / vibraphone / celesta / tubular bells

Indefinite pitch side drum / snare drum / bass drum / cymbals / (2)
triangle / tambourine / castanets / tam-tam

5 (10)

(a)

(b)

6 (a) X mediant (2)

Y leading note (2)

(b) simple (1)

triple (1)

(c) (5)

(d) false (2)

true (2)

10

7

Theory Paper   Grade 5   2018   S
Model Answers

1

(a) (i)   (3)

J. S. Bach, Cantata *Es ist euch gut*, BWV 108 (adapted)

(ii)   lower mordent   (2)

(b) (i)   Chord **A**   I 3rd / Ib   (2)

             Chord **B**   II root / IIa   (2)

(ii)   (2)

Haydn, Mass in D minor, Hob. XXII/11 (adapted)

Ic – V

or $\frac{6}{4}$ – $\frac{5}{3}$

(iii)   demisemiquaver / 32nd note   (2)

(iv)   turn / upper turn   (2)

2 (a)   augmented 4th   diminished 7th   major 6th   (6)

(b)   (4)

3   (10)

4

(a) (i)   (6)

grazioso means:		**poco rall.** means:		**a tempo** means:	
majestic	☐	getting a little quicker	☐	in time	✔
sweet	☐	getting a little louder	☐	held back	☐
graceful	✔	getting a little quieter	☐	the end	☐
very slow, solemn	☐	getting a little slower	✔	repeat from the beginning	☐

(ii) 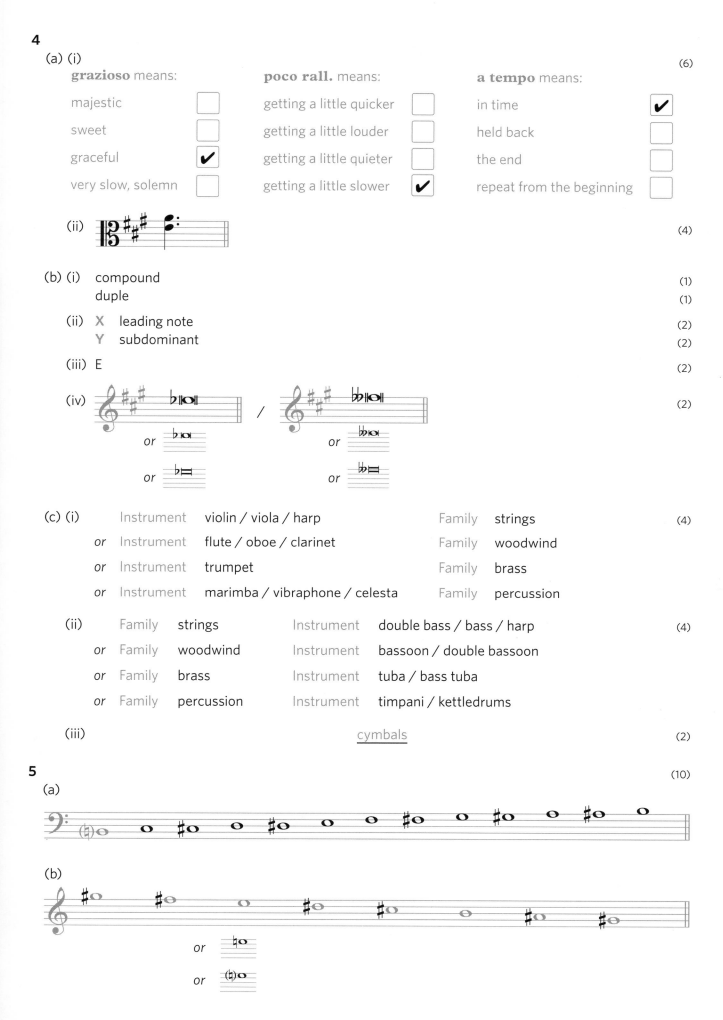   (4)

(b) (i) compound   (1)
    duple   (1)

   (ii) X leading note   (2)
         Y subdominant   (2)

   (iii) E   (2)

   (iv)   (2)

(c) (i)

	Instrument	violin / viola / harp	Family	strings
or	Instrument	flute / oboe / clarinet	Family	woodwind
or	Instrument	trumpet	Family	brass
or	Instrument	marimba / vibraphone / celesta	Family	percussion

(4)

   (ii)

	Family	strings	Instrument	double bass / bass / harp
or	Family	woodwind	Instrument	bassoon / double bassoon
or	Family	brass	Instrument	tuba / bass tuba
or	Family	percussion	Instrument	timpani / kettledrums

(4)

   (iii)   cymbals   (2)

5   (10)

(a)

(b)

6 (a) **deciso** means: (2)

delicate ☐

graceful ☐

energetic ☐

with determination ✔

(b) (2)

Finzi, No. 1 from Five Bagatelles for clarinet and piano (adapted)

(c) (4)

(d) twenty (2)

(e) (4)

(f) F sharp (1)

7 (10)

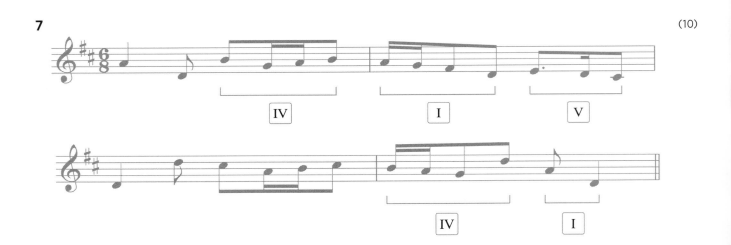

IV   I   V

IV   I

Music Theory Practice Papers 2018 Model Answers

Model answers for four practice papers, adapted from ABRSM's 2018 Music Theory exams for Grade 5

Key features:

- a list of correct answers where appropriate
- a selection of likely options where the answer can be expressed in a variety of ways
- a single exemplar where a composition-style answer is required

Support material for ABRSM Music Theory exams

Supporting the teaching and learning of music in partnership with the Royal Schools of Music

Royal Academy of Music | Royal College of Music
Royal Northern College of Music | Royal Conservatoire of Scotland

www.abrsm.org f facebook.com/abrsm
 @abrsm   ABRSM YouTube

ISBN 978-1-78601-207-4

Music Theory Practice Papers 2018 Model Answers Grade 5 ABRSM